Fearless

Suzanne D. Williams

FEARLESS

   By Suzanne D. Williams
Published by
Becky Combee Ministries, Inc.
P.O. Box 3283
Lakeland, FL 33802-3283
Beckycombeeministries.com

Unless otherwise noted, all Scripture quotations are from the King James Version of the Bible.

Albert Barnes' Notes on the Bible quotation was taken from http://www.e-sword.net

Definitions marked *Thayer's* were taken from *Thayer's Greek Definitions* from http://www.e-sword.net

Definitions marked BDB are taken from *Brown-Driver-Briggs Hebrew Definitions* from http://www.e-sword.net

Scripture quotations marked MESSAGE are taken from *The Message: The Bible in Contemporary English*, Copyright © 1993, 1994, 1995, 1996, 2000, 2001, 2002. Used by permission of NavPress Publishing Group.

Scripture quotations marked AMP are taken from the Amplified® Bible, Copyright © 1954, 1958, 1962, 1964, 1965, 1987 by The Lockman Foundation Used by permission.
(www.Lockman.org)

ISBN: 978-0-9832783-0-6

Contents

This book is dedicated to all those who prayed for me, to my mother for her guidance and support, but most especially to my husband who loved me anyway.

Thou drewest near in the day that I called upon thee: thou saidst, Fear not (La 3:27).

Foreword

*Be not thou therefore **ashamed** of
the testimony of our Lord (2Ti 1:8).*

There is life-changing power in sharing
one's testimony. (Rev 12:11) First, it is a
step of faith. To share something so
personal in public is difficult. It requires
me to move outside of my conservative
personality and trust God to help me
form the right words.

Second, it demands obedience. In
reality, I am no one special. My life has
been incredibly ordinary. Obedience
means I must do what God asks of me
no matter how small and insignificant I
feel.

The third power in giving one's
testimony lies in what it does in the
heart. When I share what God has done
in me, I become like a "city set on a hill".

The light of the gospel shines out of my life. However, it also shines into my life, exposing the work of darkness. Once exposed, the darkness has no choice but to flee. (Mt 5:14;2Co 4:4;Jn 3:20-21;Jas 4:7)

> *And they overcame him by the blood of the Lamb, and by the* **word of their testimony** *(Rev 12:11).*

In the end, my testimony isn't really about me. It's not even about what happened to me. Instead, it's about the freedom sharing it brings into my life. I've made a choice not to hide anymore. As a result, the devil no longer has any hold over me. The love and mercy of a mighty God for someone as small as I am has healed all the brokenness.

Many years before all these events transpired, I prayed over my life the words of Acts 4:29. "Lord, grant me boldness to speak your Word." I was sincere. Yet truthfully, I gave no thought afterward to the fulfillment of that prayer. Looking back now, I see this book as the result of that prayer.

I am not the same person I once was. What happened to me and the victory that came into my life through the Word of God has changed me forever. I pray that my words, in some small part, bring to you the same joy and freedom that is now mine.

God is truly good all the time!

Suzanne

Rock Bottom

My story begins by its being very normal. I grew up in a Christian home with God-fearing parents; my grandparents on both sides ministered in the church. I made good grades in school, graduated from high school with honors, married, and had a child. I never drank or smoked; I didn't do anything remotely illegal. Despite all of that, I made huge mistakes.

My biggest mistake was my loss of self-control. Over a period of many years, I stewed in anger. It seemed I was always upset about something. Easily slighted, I eventually alienated myself from my friends until I was alone, bitter, and miserable. Oh outwardly, I seemed fine. I smiled and did what was asked of me, but in my heart, I was very unhappy.

I remember hating myself for the dark thoughts that entered my mind. I tried overcoming them on my own. I bottled my anger inside and told myself, "As long as I act okay, no one will know how upset I am and no one will get hurt." The truth is, my hatred was not hurting them; it was hurting ME.

Ultimately, I reaped exactly what I had sown. This is a scriptural principle, and though it works in the positive, it also works in the negative. The apostle Paul said, "For he that soweth to his flesh shall of the flesh reap corruption." (Gal 6:8) I can express it no better than that.

In 2007, my normal world fell apart. I found myself gripped by immense fear. On a trip to a local theme park, I collapsed on the pavement unable to breathe. Immediately, terror and great confusion filled my mind. For two solid hours, I sat there gasping for air, unable to stand, trying not to scream.

Afterward, I couldn't shake off the fear from that event. As the days crept by, it gradually gained hold over my mind. I gave into it with my emotions. I allowed it to make my decisions. The Scripture in Deuteronomy 28:67 exactly describes my state of mind. In the morning, I wished for night. At night, I wished for morning.

Eventually, my physical health failed. I couldn't eat. What I did eat I couldn't hold down. I was nauseous all the time. I stopped going out to dinner; it was just too hard. I gave up on enjoying a meal; what did it matter anyway?

I suffered secretly, going out of my way to hide it from everyone. I told my spouse I was fine. I promised to attend things, knowing I'd back out at the last minute. I used every excuse in the book. I'd say I had a "bad stomach" or was "too tired." In the process, I began to create a mental list of places where I would never return. Over time, my list became so long that I stopped leaving home. Going to the store became impossible, and I dragged myself to church.

Sometime in September, I hit rock bottom. Hitting rock bottom in life leaves you with an entirely new perspective. I could see my life was a mess. My personal attempts to "fix" things had resulted in complete failure. I was desperate for a cure.

When you are at the bottom, when you reach that point of complete desperation, you finally know where your answer is. At that moment, I was as empty and as far down as anyone could ever get. The only one place left to look was up. One afternoon, I fell on my face and cried out to God. "FIX ME! I will do ANYTHING, anything at all if you will just fix me!"

I meant every word. In my searching on my own for solutions, I met people who suffered as I did; it was frightening how long they had suffered, some of them for many, many years. They had no hope for a cure. In my heart, that just wasn't good enough. I didn't want a patch or a pill to cover things up. I didn't want to "survive." No, I wanted complete freedom. I wanted to never think like that again, to never suffer physically again. I wanted something that seemed so distant—I wanted to leave home without a care in the world.

I sit here today exactly that free. I found my cure in the Word of God. I found it sitting in God's presence. However, my healing was as gradual as my descent was. There was never a point where a bright light shown from heaven and suddenly everything was all right. What took me years to accumulate, took me years to overcome.

I always say my testimony is a mobile one because I walk it out every day. Daily I lean my faith and trust on Jesus Christ. I lean on Christ, and I obey.

My healing came through obedience. I had to do what I had said, in that desperate moment, that I would do and do it unquestioning. When God instructed me to apologize to certain people, I did it. When He told me to bury myself in the Bible, to give up certain things of secular society, I did it. With every step I made, I grew more and more able to hear His "still, small voice" and to know what next was required of me. (1Ki 19:12)

It took me a long time to realize I was well. I remember when it hit me. I was working on a project at church with a girl who didn't know me, who hadn't heard my story. She didn't know how hard it had been to agree to work on that project, nor what a step of faith it was to say "yes" when I was asked. As we sat there doing our job, she turned to me and said, "I wanted to work with you because you're so calm." Imagine that! Someone had called me calm!

I remember my response. I said, "You know your weakest point often becomes your strongest." With those words, I knew I had turned a corner.

God has restored my health, my strength, and my confidence. He even healed my emotions and repaired my social life, two things I hadn't asked for. All I had asked for was to leave home again. For God, that wasn't good enough. He had bigger plans. God's plans are always higher, wider, and broader than whatever we can possibly dream. (Eph 3:18)

God's desire was for me to be completely fearless–fearless, full of faith, and free!

God wants you well

*For **God hath not** given us the spirit of fear; but of power, and of love, and of a sound mind (2Ti 1:7).*

The most essential truth for you to place in your heart is that God did not do this to you. It was never His desire for you to suffer the torment of fear. (1Jn 4:18) The Scripture in 2 Timothy 1:7 is definite about that. "God has not" means "God has not." There is no room for any other interpretation.

Fear and the mental degradation of fear are demonic. They are not from God. The Bible tells us in 1 Corinthians 14:3 that "God is not the author of confusion, but of peace." Here is a straightforward truth! Any confusion in my mind is not from God. God didn't give that to me! God gives peace!

God's will for man can also be seen in John 10:10. Here, Jesus said, "The thief cometh not, but for to steal, and to kill, and to destroy: I am come that they might have **life**, and that they might have it **more abundantly**." Jesus came to earth and died on a cruel cross to bring abundant, bountiful, generous life! That which steals, kills, and destroys is NOT abundance! This includes fear! It really is that simple.

Know the enemy

> Be well balanced (temperate, sober of mind), be vigilant and cautious at all times; for that **enemy of yours, the devil**, roams around like a lion roaring [in fierce hunger], seeking someone to seize upon and devour (1Pe 5:8 AMP).

Jesus wanted you to know who the real enemy is. It seems like common sense to say that a soldier who doesn't know what side he's on cannot properly fight a battle. Well, our enemy is the thief, the devil. The devil is responsible for fear, panic, anxiety, and terror. Until you know this fact, you will be unable to fight against him.

Too many Christians accept sickness, hardship, and stress as something God is using to teach them, but this is not scriptural. (Jas 1:13) Instead, the Bible states that the Holy Spirit and the Word of God are our teachers. (Jn 14:26;2Ti 3:16) We learn and grow as we spend time meditating and abiding in God's Word. (Eph 4:15;1Pe 2:2)

Truth, wisdom, and good gifts come from God! (Jas 1:17) The devil, on the other hand, is the father, the originator, of lies. Jesus told this in John 8:44. Speaking to the Pharisees, He stated, "Ye are of your father the devil, and the lusts of your father ye will do. He was a murderer from the beginning, and

abode not in the truth, because there is **no truth in him**. When he speaketh a lie, he speaketh of his own: for **he is a liar, and the father of it.**" (Jn 8:44) Wow! Just think! Every tormenting, terror-filled, and panicked thought that floats through your head is a lie! Our Savior said there is NO TRUTH in them. NONE!

God's will

God's will for man regarding health is found in a beautiful passage of Scripture, Isaiah 53. I want to concentrate on verse 4.

> *Surely he [Jesus] hath borne our **griefs**, and carried our **sorrows**: yet we did esteem him stricken, smitten of God, and afflicted (Isa 53:4).*

Notice the two words, "griefs" and "sorrows. The study reference, *Albert*

Barnes' Notes on the Bible, gives an excellent definition of these two words.

> *"Perhaps the proper difference between this word [sorrows] and the word translated griefs is, that this [sorrows] refers to pains of the mind, that [griefs] of the body; this to anguish, anxiety, or trouble of the soul; that to bodily infirmity and disease."*

In the original Hebrew, the word "griefs" specifically means sickness of the body and "sorrows" refers to mental anguish. We see from this verse that Jesus in His death on the cross not only cleansed man of sin, but carried away sicknesses and mental anguish too. He bore all the lies and torments of the devil onto Himself so that we would not have to bear them.

With His death and resurrection, Jesus defeated the devil once and for all. (Col

2:15) I love His words in John 16:33. "These things I have spoken unto you, that **in me ye might have peace**. In the world ye shall have tribulation: but be of good cheer; **I have overcome the world.**" Given Jesus' sacrifice, why should we continue to struggle against something His death and resurrection has overcome?

The Word of God says there is no darkness in God, not even a shadow! (Jas 1:17;1Jn 1:5) Instead, the prince of the kingdom of darkness is Satan, and God is the father of light. (Col 1:13) Jesus came to earth to shine forth life and light onto any who would believe! (Jn 1:4;Jn 3:16) Death, sin, sickness, and mental anguish, all of these, have no place in the life of God's children. We no longer have to be afraid!

Forgiveness

*For as the heaven is high above the earth, so great is his mercy toward them that fear him. As far as the east is from the west, **so far hath he removed** our transgressions from us (Ps 103:11-12).*

The second truth you must embrace to become completely free of fear's torment is forgiveness. You must forgive others and you must forgive yourself.

Sometimes the hardest person to forgive is yourself. I know when I began my journey toward healing, I wasted considerable time blaming myself. Each time I collapsed back into fear, I felt like such a failure. Over and over I asked, "Why can't I conquer this?"

The truth was that "I" couldn't conquer it at all. "I" had royally messed things up. To banish fear from my life forever, I had to dispense with my guilt and accept God's forgiveness each time I fell apart.

God is a loving God. He is a merciful God. In fact, Ephesians 2:4 says He is "rich in mercy." Think of that! Rich! This means He has more than we'll ever need. No matter how horrible we've been, no matter how weak or stubborn, He is more than enough.

We find the proof through Jesus' death and resurrection. The Bible says, "But God shows and clearly proves His [own] love for us by the fact that while we were still sinners, Christ (the Messiah, the Anointed One) died for us." (Ro 5:8 AMP) Notice, it says, "WHILE" we were sinners, Jesus died. He didn't wait for us to admit our sin. In fact, we didn't deserve rescue.

I didn't deserve forgiveness for all the hatred in my heart. I didn't deserve God coming down to where I was and lifting me up out of the mire. (Ps 40:1-2) Yet that's what He did, and He did it because His love for me was so very much.

Asking Forgiveness

As much as God loved us, we must love and forgive others to the same extent. Where it is needed, we must ask others to forgive us for our hurtful behavior. In return, we must forgive them for any of theirs.

Mark 11:25 says, "And when ye stand praying, forgive...that your Father...may forgive you." With unforgiveness in our heart, our prayers are vain. They fall empty and powerless. In order to be free, we must repent and forgive.

For me, the forgiveness I needed was for my own behavior. There were people who knew I was angry with them. For years, I had avoided speaking to them. When I at last grasped this principle, I called each one and said, "I'm sorry. I was wrong." I didn't care anymore what I looked like because my focus was now on getting well.

There is no embarrassment in humbling yourself and asking for forgiveness. In fact, the Word of God says, "Humble yourselves in the sight of the Lord, and he shall lift you up." The "lifting" comes after the humility.

Salvation

God is so good and so faithful. He loves you so very much. He has forgiven you for all your errors and mistakes. All that is required to receive His forgiveness is your prayer.

Pray these words:

"Father, I come to you today in need of what your plan of salvation has provided for me. I need your health and joy. I choose to believe, right now, that Jesus died for me, to cleanse my sins AND to give to me everything I need to live a peaceful, abundant life. Come into my heart, wash me, make me new, and guide me through your Word into the fullness of what Jesus' death has given. Thank you, Father. I believe. Amen."

Finding Forgetfulness

> Brethren, I count not myself to
> have apprehended: but this one
> thing I do, **forgetting those things
> which are behind**, and reaching
> forth unto those things which are
> before (Php 3:13).

To move forward out of the grasp of
fear, you first must forget. In fact, you
will not find health and freedom until
you do. It's that important.

Forgetting was the one thing I wanted
the most desperately. I wanted to forget
how to react to my circumstances out of
fear. My mind had become so confused
that I actually couldn't remember how
to be unafraid.

Now, it is important to know what the
Bible means by forgetting. *Thayer's*

Greek Definitions defines the word "forgetting" as "no longer caring for." This is what I really wanted. I didn't want to care about fear.

It's not that I expected to get up the next morning and not remember what had happened to me. That is unrealistic. No, I still remember everything or I couldn't write this book. Instead, I wanted my reactions to be without fear.

Forgetting is a process of the mind. It is the result of the thoughts we choose to think. We see this in several places in the Bible. I particularly like a verse in Hebrews 11. This chapter in Hebrews lists what many call the "fathers" of our faith. These are the people whose lives we describe to our children. However, notice what it says about these people in verse 15.

> And truly, *if they had been mindful* of that country from

*whence they came out, they might have **had opportunity** to have returned (Heb 11:15).*

Even these great men of God had a choice to make. Finding himself in the midst of a strange land, Abraham could have thought about the benefits of returning to Ur. Noah, on the ark out of the sight of any land, could have despaired, especially when that first dove returned. Each person listed here could have chosen not to forget. They could have chosen to remember their past. However, the Bible says, if they did, an opportunity to return would come. The opportunity to go back into their bondage came as they thought about the past.

The Bible tells us this about the children of Israel as well. In Numbers 11:5, they mourned the lack of leeks, onions, and garlic they'd had when they were in the land of Egypt. Imagine that! Here they were, delivered from the bondage of slavery in such a mighty way with amazing signs and wonders, and they thought about going back into slavery for the food!

God's Part

This may surprise you, but God does have a part to play. You are not alone. Proverbs 16:3 states, "Commit thy works unto the Lord, and thy thoughts shall be established." That word "established" means "to be fixed, stable." (H3559 BDB) Our part is committing our thoughts to the Lord. God's part is securing them.

What we often don't realize is that forgetting is supernatural. Like forgiving, it is not something you do under your own power. Instead, we fully surrender to God and place our trust in Him to do what He has promised. The good news is He WILL do it. We have only to do what is asked of us. (Nu 23:19;1Ki 8:56; Ps 119:89)

We are asked to be like God, and the Bible says He forgets. We read this in Isaiah 43:25 where God says, "I, *even* I, *am* he that blotteth out thy transgressions for mine own sake, and **will not remember** thy sins." We as children of God must follow His actions. To be like Him then, we must also strive to forget. (Eph 5:1)

The Price

The reason forgetting is so important is because of the heavy price we pay for NOT forgetting. We already read in Hebrews 11 that not forgetting causes a return to bondage. That is the first price. In the very next chapter, Hebrews 12:15, we read a second price.

*Follow peace with all men...**looking diligently** lest any man fail of the grace of God; lest any root of bitterness springing up trouble you, and thereby many be defiled (Heb 12:14-15).*

"Looking diligently" means we are always looking. We never take a break; we never stop. We look for peace all the time because forgetting to look causes us to fall behind in God's grace. This results in a terrible bitterness that destroys our family, our friends, and ourselves. That is a high cost!

Ezekiel 23:19 details a third price. Here it says remembering the past "multiplied" the problem. Oh, how true this is! Every time I allow my mind to dwell on fear, the fear only grows larger. In consequence, I become like the fourth price, unfruitful.

In the parable of the seed and the sower, Jesus states that God's Word is like a seed. Planted among thorns, all the cares of life grow up around it, and it chokes, yielding no fruit. (Lk 8:14)

Allowing the cares of life, in this case the fear, to operate in my mind causes any seed of God's Word planted in my heart to never do what it was planted to do. It causes me to lack fruit. All my actions are vain. Poor is the farmer whose harvest is lost to the weeds!

Not a Trace

Below are two Scriptures about forgetting that sum up God's will for man. It is God's will that "not a trace" of the memory of this fear remain. Instead, we remember the power of the Lord, which brings our deliverance. How amazing and marvelous is that?

Make these verses your confession!

*When you go out looking for your old adversaries you won't find them—**Not a trace** of your old enemies, **not even a memory**. That's right. Because I, your God, have a firm grip on you and I'm not letting go. I'm telling you, 'Don't panic. I'm right here to help you.' (Isa 41:11-13* THE MESSAGE*)*

*They [the former tyrant masters] are dead, they shall not live and reappear; they are **powerless** ghosts, they **shall not rise and come back**. Therefore You have visited and made an end of them and **caused every memory of them [every trace** of their supremacy] to perish (Isa 26:14 AMP).*

Renewing the Mind

> *And be not conformed to this world: but be ye **transformed** by the **renewing of your mind**, that ye may prove what is that good, and acceptable, and perfect, will of God (Ro 12:2).*

Man is a spirit; he has a soul, and he lives in a body. (1Th 5:23) Salvation creates in man a brand new spirit. (Eze 11:19) All the old things of the past are gone and all things of the spirit are now new. (2Co 5:17) However, the Bible in Romans 12 tells us that the habits and thinking processes of the mind remain the same. Change, or transformation, only occurs through renewal of the mind.

The unrenewed mind is what causes our problems. I received salvation as a young girl, and at that time, my spirit man was recreated. Yet I still spent the greater part of my life thinking "unrenewed." I listened to any thought that came into my head. Worse yet, I voiced them. Then, when fear became my primary thought, I found myself completely crippled. I didn't know how else to think.

Who hasn't begged God at some point in their life to shut off the thoughts in their head? I know I did many times. I wanted an empty mind, but there is no such thing as an empty mind. Your mind will always be full of something.

My walk towards freedom from the negative thoughts of fear began when I realized what renewing the mind actually required. Renewing the mind is a deliberate action. It means thinking about what you are thinking about! When we renew our mind, we essentially fill it with so much of God

that His words crowd out all the
thoughts the devil tries to place there.

God's thoughts are always stronger than
the devil's. (Isa 55:9) I like the
illustration of the Scripture in Ephesians
5:26, "That He [Christ] might sanctify
and cleanse it [the church] with the
washing of water by the word." Each
time I voice a Scripture, God's Word,
like a gentle ocean wave, "washes" and
cleanses my mind. God's words in me
effectively rinse the filth of fear from my
thinking.

What You Speak

> Therefore take no thought, **saying**
> (Mt 6:31).

It is speaking God's Word that washes
my mind. Frequently, I am asked what I
did daily to overcome the thoughts of
fear. Matthew 6:31 supplies the answer.
In this verse, we learn how we "take"

thoughts. We take them when we speak them. Every time we speak the thought – "I am so afraid. What if something happens to me?" – we make a choice to accept that thought. Our acceptance of the thought then gives it power in our life.

This works both positively and negatively. The Bible speaks many times about the strength of our confession. Our confession brings to us God's great salvation, but our confession also has the power to hold us in bondage. (Pr 6:2;Pr 18:21;Ro 10:10) The Scriptures in James 3:6 refer to the tongue as "a fire, a world of iniquity." This is a powerful analogy to the strength of our words!

The solution to renewing the mind against fear then is simple. Stop speaking the fear! At no point is the devil going to cease placing his negative thoughts into your head as long as you voice them. In fact, every time you do, you keep yourself enslaved.

Freedom begins with what you speak. You speak the thoughts of God instead of the thoughts of fear. It's not enough to think positive thoughts. It takes a deliberate action. You must speak God's Word for victory to come.

The thought comes into your mind, "You know you can't do this. You will fall apart."

However, you speak, "Greater is He who is in me!" (1Jn 4:4)

One second later, another thought creeps in. "You are going to collapse and get sick again."

But you voice, "God is my strength. I am able!"(Ps 27:1;Ps 46:1-3;Php 4:13) Minute by minute, hour by hour, this is how the battle is won.

You know though, in the beginning I didn't really believe what I said. It was as I meditated on and spoke God's words continually that they registered in my heart. My spirit man heard the words and the words changed my thinking.

Speaking the right thoughts instead of the wrong ones is like any learned skill. I learned how to type by first concentrating on the keys. I took deliberate steps to remember where to place my fingers. The more I practiced, the more time I spent typing, the easier it became, the more "second nature" it was for me. Now I can type quickly without looking at the keyboard at all. What wasn't a habit became one through patience and dedication.

Renewing the mind works this same way. A habit of speaking fear changes to a habit of speaking the Word as I practice it. In the process, the thoughts of the devil lose their power over my mind.

This is faith. (Heb 11:1) We speak over our lives those things that are not in our lives, and the power of God honors our words and moves the mountain of fear! (Mt 17:20;Mk 11:23-24)

Peace in God's Presence

*Peace I leave with you, my peace I give unto you: not as the world giveth, give I unto you. **Let not your heart be troubled, neither let it be afraid** (Jn 14:27).*

When I was at my lowest point, the thing I desired the most was peace in my mind and rest for my body. Shaking and trembling, nauseous and confused, I wanted the torment to end. Simple things like enjoying my garden seemed as hard as climbing the tallest mountain.

I found peace sitting in God's presence. During my most desperate moments, I began playing worship music. As I listened to the songs, sometimes for hours, God's presence filled the room. Soon, the words also began flowing from my heart.

Though I didn't realize it at the time, this is a spiritual law. Romans 8:6 proclaims, "For to be carnally minded *is* death; but **to be spiritually minded *is* life and peace**." When I worship God, I become "spiritually minded." Worship shifts my mental focus away from the thoughts of fear onto God.

It also bypasses the work of the mind. Where my mind may be in turmoil, worship comes from the spirit man. (Jn 4:23-24) I believe hearing the Word worked more to bring peace and clarity at those times when my mind was simply unable to grasp thoughts through reading.

The truth is fear cannot stay in the presence of God. Isaiah 10:27 states, "The yoke shall be destroyed **because of the anointing**." The anointing in the presence of God breaks the bondage of the devil. (Lk 4:18)

However, there is an even greater truth. Yes, God's anointing removes fear (bringing peace) but God's anointing also prevents fear. I can remain out from underneath fear by taking time every day, no matter how well I feel that day, to worship God.

Complete

> *Thou wilt **keep** him in perfect peace, whose mind is stayed on thee: because he trusteth in thee (Isa 26:3).*

> *And the peace of God, which passeth all understanding, shall **keep** your hearts and minds through Christ Jesus (Php 4:7).*

When I worship God, when I "stay" my mind on Him, I place myself in His presence. I in effect "keep" myself in His peace.

"Keep" is an important word in these verses because in both the Hebrew and Greek texts it means "to guard." (G5342, *Thayer's*, H5341, BDB) God's peace guards, or protects, my heart and my mind. (Jn 16:33)

Yet what is peace? The definition of the word "peace" in these texts further helps our understanding of God's promise. In the Greek, "peace" means "a state of tranquility, exemption from the rage and havoc of war, harmony, security, safety, and prosperity." (G1515, *Thayer's*) The Hebrew expands this to include "completeness, soundness, welfare, health, and contentment." (H7965, BDB)

God's peace is COMPLETE peace! It is all-encompassing. Nothing that we need has been left out – nothing! If you think about that, what would peace be if certain aspects were missing? Where is the peace for someone in great debt, if he cannot believe in peace for his finances? Where is the peace for someone with marital troubles, if God left peace out of marriage?

God never does things halfway. His greatest desire for man is a long life and eternal salvation. (Ps 91:16) We should not expect anything less from His great love for us. Love as big as God's just gives and gives and gives. (Ro 5:8)

I think Romans 8:35-39 says this best.

> *Who shall separate us from the love of Christ? shall tribulation, or distress, or persecution, or famine, or nakedness, or peril, or sword? As it is written, For thy sake we are killed all the day long; we are accounted as sheep for the slaughter. Nay, in all these things we are more than conquerors through him that loved us. For I am persuaded, that neither death,*

*nor life, nor angels, nor principalities, nor powers, nor things present, nor things to come, Nor height, nor depth, nor any other creature, **shall be able to separate us from the love of God**, which is in Christ Jesus our Lord.*

Strength and Power

*Finally, my brethren, **be strong in the Lord**, and in the power of his might (Eph 6:10).*

Finding peace was essential to my recovery, but increasing my strength was needful to prevent falling back into fear. In the natural, an athlete is only as strong as the time he spent in training. A marathon runner cannot complete a race without first strengthening himself for the task.

In 1 Corinthians 3:1, the apostle Paul referred to the church at Corinth as "babes in Christ." Well, babies are not strong enough to withstand things like a toddler, and a toddler cannot withstand the things of an adult. Paul applies this analogy to our spiritual lives. Until I am spiritually strong, I will continue to fall prey to the bondage of the devil.

So how do we become strong? Strength, healing, and restoration come through the power of God, through the person of the Holy Spirit. (Eph 6:10) No matter how weak I feel in my flesh or my mind, because the Holy Spirit's power is in me I can walk upright. (Eph 3:16)

John 14:26 in the *Amplified Bible* specifically describes this role of the Holy Spirit for those who have Christ.

> *But the Comforter (Counselor, Helper, Intercessor, Advocate, **Strengthener**, Standby), the Holy Spirit, Whom the Father will send in My name..."*

The Holy Ghost, or Holy Spirit, is our strength. Strengthening is actually His job!

Praying in the Spirit

> *But ye, beloved, **building up yourselves** on your most holy faith, **praying** in the Holy Ghost (Jude 1:20).*

We draw from the strength of the Holy Spirit (Holy Ghost) through time spent praying in other tongues. First Corinthians 14:4 confirms this. It states, "He that speaketh in an *unknown* tongue **edifieth himself**."The word "edify" here means "to build up from the foundation." (*Thayer's*) I like that definition because without a good foundation, a house will fall. Well, the Word of God says Jesus is our foundation. (Lk 6:48) Our spiritual house stands against the winds and the rains of life when we have a strong foundation. One way we build our strong foundation is through praying in tongues.

Praying in tongues is also important because it aids a troubled mind. During a moment of terror, your mind is a hindrance. I know there were times when I couldn't have told you my name. I was that confused. However, when I pray in tongues, the Holy Spirit prays with me. (Ro 8:26) His words speak directly to God, bypassing the confusion in my mind and overriding the weakness in my flesh.

The Holy Spirit also prays the perfect will of God for me. With His help in prayer, God's power is released in my life exactly where I need it. (Ro 8:27) The book of James describes the power of Holy Spirit-led prayer.

> *The earnest (heartfelt, continued) prayer of a righteous man **makes tremendous power available** [dynamic in its working] (Jas 5:16 AMP).*

Earnest, dedicated, sincere prayer from a child of God brings Holy Spirit power onto the scene. More than just words, prayer draws on God's strength, His power, to work in me and change my situation.

Prayer is about freedom from yesterday's trauma and prevention of future difficulties. We must move from desperation, God fixing what is wrong in us, into a determination to keep ourselves strong. Praying in the spirit is a very important scriptural tool to build strength.

But there is yet another benefit to a life of prayer! Through prayer, we learn to recognize God's voice. (Jn 10:27) In our times of prayer, we fellowship with the Father. We come to know Him, and He then changes our heart and mind forever! (Jn 14:7;Jn 14:17;1Jn 1:3) No longer do we fall prey to the weakness of fear!

Go Anyway

*For ye shall **go out with joy**, and **be led forth with peace**: the mountains and the hills shall break forth before you into singing, and all the trees of the field shall clap their hands (Isa 55:12).*

Overcoming fear was the hardest thing I've ever done because it required me to do the very thing I feared the most. The fact is that there isn't any way to walk around fear. You must face it head on. (Ex 14:13;Ps 91:8;Eph 6:16)

But there is good news! We do not go alone nor do we go without God's promise going with us. (Mt 28:20) I especially love the Scripture in Isaiah 55 because it speaks of going, but going in great joy. I know at my most difficult moments, when I had to "go anyway," I toted this verse with me in my heart.

In the story of the woman with the issue of blood, Jesus spoke this same promise. He said, "**Go in peace** and be whole." (Mk 5:34;Lk 8:48) Notice He said more than just, "Go"; He assured her she would also go peacefully!

In order to be well, she had to take action. The Bible says she had already seen many physicians, so she could have given up and stayed home. If she had though, she would never have received her healing.

The Scripture says that instead she sought Him out. (Mk 5:28) Despite what was happening in her body, despite how she felt, she went out looking for the Christ! Like her, to become free, no matter how large our fear is, we have to determine to leave home, trusting in God to help us. We must "go anyway."

Stop making excuses!

Sometimes doing what seems safe is the wrong thing to do. In my case, staying at home was comfortable, both to my personality and because of the fear that gripped me when I left. However, staying at home only placed me in further bondage.

There came a point when I had to stop making excuses. I had to agree to "go" and dedicate myself to completing the task no matter what. I had to stop constantly backing out. I won't lie to you. It was very hard. There were times when I went falling completely apart. However, the more I went, the more I was able to go and in greater peace.

I learned I could rely on the people who loved me to take me. I knew I was not strong enough mentally or physically to go on my own without giving up and coming home. Left alone, I would have returned, given I even got out the door.

You have to start by depending on people. Often, I told my husband to go but refuse to turn around. I relied on him to take me there. But I knew all along that as I grew stronger and healthier, I would do things on my own. I knew I could not always have others "bail me out." Until then, I went on the power of other people. It was three years before I traveled alone. When I did, I rejoiced, knowing God in me had won the battle over fear.

I don't know what your particular fear is. I have talked to people with very different fearful thoughts. Yet the principles of the Word of God remain the same. God says, "Fear not. Go in peace. Go rejoicing," so that is what we have to do! When we do, He honors His promises and our life begins to change.

Jesus said we were never alone. (Mt 28:20) At no point, do we have to walk desolate, outside of Him. Instead, He has promised to guide our footsteps, to light the path before us, and help us walk out of bondage into freedom and victory! (Pr 3:25-26;Pr 16:9;Pr 4:18)

Prepare Yourself

When you're facing fear, fear seems huge. It looks like it will consume everything around you. Remember, this is a lie!

The truth is God is so much bigger than fear. He is SO MUCH BIGGER than fear!

Being able to walk through whatever your fear is comes with preparation. (Ps 23:4;Is 43:2) When I know I have to do something particularly difficult, I get up as early as necessary and prepare my heart, my spirit man, in advance. This gives me the strength I need to do the task.

Preparation means I am ready for whatever comes my way. No longer am I weak, but through time spent in prayer, worship, and meditation in the Scriptures, I constantly remind myself of who God is and place His "bigness" in my heart.

In the next chapter, I have listed some of my favorite Scriptures about our great God. Dedicate yourself today to read and study them. As you do, when fear comes, instead of collapsing, your spirit man will rise up and say, "I can do this! God is BIG. He is bigger than this fear! He loves me, and I can do this!" (Php 4:13)

Think about our mighty God today!

God Is

Able

And when he was come into the house,
the blind men came to him: and Jesus
saith unto them, Believe ye that **I am
able** to do this? They said unto him, Yea,
Lord (Mt 9:28).

And now, brethren, I commend you to
God, and to the word of his grace,
which is able to build you up, and to
give you an inheritance among all them
which are sanctified (Ac 20:32).

And **God is able** to make all grace
abound toward you; that ye, always
having all sufficiency in all things, may
abound to every good work (2Co 9:8).

Wherefore **he is able** also to save them
to the uttermost that come unto God by

him, seeing he ever liveth to make intercession for them (Heb 7:25).

Faithful

Know therefore that the Lord thy God, he is God, **the faithful God**, which keepeth covenant and mercy with them that love him and keep his commandments to a thousand generations (Dt 7:9).

Thy mercy, O Lord, is in the heavens; and thy **faithfulness** reacheth unto the clouds (Ps 36:5).

God is faithful, by whom ye were called unto the fellowship of his Son Jesus Christ our Lord (1Co 1:9).

Let us hold fast the profession of our faith without wavering; (for **he is faithful** that promised) (Heb 10:23).

Faithful is he that calleth you, who also will do it (1Th 5:24).

Forever the same

For I am the Lord, I **change not** (Mal 3:6a).

But unto the Son he saith, Thy throne, O God, is **for ever and ever**: a sceptre of righteousness is the sceptre of thy kingdom (Heb 1:8).

Jesus Christ **the same** yesterday, and to day, and **for ever** (Heb 13:8).

Being born again, not of corruptible seed, but of incorruptible, by the word of God, which **liveth and abideth for ever** (1Pe 1:23).

Great

For **great** is the Lord, and greatly to be praised: he also is to be feared above all gods (1Ch 16:25).

For the Lord is a **great** God, and a **great** King above all gods (Ps 95:3).

Great is the Lord, and greatly to be praised; and his **greatness** is unsearchable (Ps 145:3).

He shall be **great**, and shall be called the Son of the Highest: and the Lord God shall give unto him the throne of his father David (Lk 1:32).

Higher

For thou, Lord, art **high above** all the earth: thou art exalted far above all gods (Ps 97:9).

The Lord is **high above** all nations, and his glory above the heavens (Ps 113:4).

For as the heavens are higher than the earth, so are my ways **higher** than your ways, and my thoughts than your thoughts (Isa 55:9).

He that cometh from above is **above all**: he that is of the earth is earthly, and speaketh of the earth: he that cometh from heaven is **above all** (Jn 3:31).

For such an high priest became us, who is holy, harmless, undefiled, separate from sinners, and made **higher** than the heavens (Heb 7:26).

Living

I make a decree, That in every dominion of my kingdom men tremble and fear before the God of Daniel: for he is the **living God**, and stedfast for ever, and his kingdom that which shall not be destroyed, and his dominion shall be even unto the end (Da 6:26).

And Simon Peter answered and said, Thou art the Christ, the Son of the **living God** (Mt 16:16).

And what agreement hath the temple of God with idols? for ye are the temple of the **living God**; as God hath said, I will dwell in them, and walk in them; and I will be their God, and they shall be my people (2Co 6:16).

I am he that **liveth**, and was dead; and, behold, I am **alive** for evermore, Amen;

and have the keys of hell and of death
(Rev 1:18).

Merciful

But thou, O Lord, art a God full of
compassion, and gracious,
longsuffering, and **plenteous in mercy**
and truth (Ps 86:15).

The Lord is gracious, and full of
compassion; slow to anger, and **of great
mercy**. The Lord is good to all: and his
tender mercies are over all his works (Ps
145:8-9).

But God, who is **rich in mercy**, for his
great love wherewith he loved us (Eph
2:4).

Blessed be the God and Father of our
Lord Jesus Christ, which according to his
abundant mercy hath begotten us again

unto a lively hope by the resurrection of Jesus Christ from the dead (1Pe 1:3).

Powerful

Great is our Lord, and of **great power**: his understanding is infinite (Ps 147:5).

How God anointed Jesus of Nazareth with the Holy Ghost and with **power**: who went about doing good, and healing all that were oppressed of the devil; for God was with him (Ac 10:38).

For I am not ashamed of the gospel of Christ: for it is the **power of God** unto salvation to every one that believeth; to the Jew first, and also to the Greek (Ro 1:16).

Finally, my brethren, be strong in the Lord, and in the **power of his might** (Eph 6:10).

Saying, We give thee thanks, O Lord God Almighty, which art, and wast, and art to come; because thou hast taken to thee thy **great power**, and hast reigned (Rev 11:17).

Strong

Now these are thy servants and thy people, whom thou hast redeemed by thy great power, and by thy **strong hand** (Ne 1:10).

Now know I that the Lord saveth his anointed; he will hear him from his holy heaven with the **saving strength** of his right hand (Ps 20:6).

The Lord is their **strength**, and he is the **saving strength** of his anointed (Ps 28:8).

Behold, the Lord GOD will come with **strong hand**, and his arm shall rule for him: behold, his reward is with him, and his work before him (Isa 40:10).

Lift up your eyes on high, and behold who hath created these things, that bringeth out their host by number: he calleth them all by names by the greatness of his might, for that **he is strong** in power; not one faileth (Isa 40:26).

Because the foolishness of God is wiser than men; and the weakness of **God is stronger** than men (1Co 1:25).

Willing

He shall call upon me, and **I will** answer him: **I will** be with him in trouble; **I will** deliver him, and honour him (Ps 91:15).

For I the Lord thy God will hold thy right hand, saying unto thee, Fear not; **I will** help thee (Isa 41:13).

Behold, **I will do** a new thing; now it shall spring forth; shall ye not know it? **I will** even make a way in the wilderness, and rivers in the desert (Isa 43:19).

For the Lord **GOD will help me**; therefore shall I not be confounded: therefore have I set my face like a flint, and I know that I shall not be ashamed (Isa 50:7).

Then the heathen that are left round about you shall know that I the Lord build the ruined places, and plant that that was desolate: I the Lord have spoken it, and **I will do it** (Eze 36:36).

If ye shall ask any thing in my name, **I will do it** (Jn 14:14).

Hope

*Christ in you, **the hope** of glory
(Col 1:27).*

The ultimate purpose of this book is to give you hope that your life can change. When I was at the bottom, I remember how hopeless it seemed. I felt trapped in some endless cycle of despair and misery. Those were dark days.

Hope returned when I realized "Christ in me" made the difference. I am in myself not a strong person. I am not particularly wise. I have no talent for making speeches. However, "in Christ" I am somebody. In Christ, I am strong, righteous, and able.

The truth is "Christ in me" did the work. (Jn 14:10) He made the change. When I gave up being "myself" and instead determined to be only what He asked of me, I began to see light in the darkness.

Those "in Christ" are provided many wonderful things. Redemption is free "in Christ." (Ro 3:24) There is no more condemnation for our sin "in Christ." (Ro 8:1) "In Christ" we are free from the power of death. (Ro 8:2)

"In Christ" we are set apart from the world. (1Co 1:2) "In Christ" we have wisdom. (1Co 1:30) "In Christ" we have purpose and grace. (2Ti 1:9) The list goes on.

It is learning who God has made me to be in Christ that brings hope. Romans 5:2 states it this way, "By whom [Jesus Christ] also we have access by faith into this grace wherein we **stand, and rejoice in hope** of the glory of God." I like that! In Christ, we can stand again, this time rejoicing. In Christ, we find hope and fearless, joyful life. (Eph 6:14)

My prayer for you today is that you will have what I now have. I believe one day as you work around your house or have lunch with a friend, one day when you are doing something so seemingly ordinary, you'll look up and say, "You know what? I am so happy!"

That, my dear friend, is what life "in Christ" is all about — It is continual joy and peace in believing! (Ro 15:13)

> *Then he said unto them, Go your way, eat the fat, and drink the sweet, and send portions unto them for whom nothing is prepared: for this day is holy unto our Lord: neither be ye sorry;* ***for the joy of the Lord is your strength*** *(Ne 8:10).*

Promises for the Mind

Thou shalt **not be afraid** for the terror by night; nor for the arrow that flieth by day (Ps 91:5).

He shall **not be afraid** of evil tidings: his heart is fixed, trusting in the Lord (Ps 112:7).

Trust in the Lord with all thine heart; and **lean not unto thine own understanding**. In all thy ways acknowledge him, and he shall direct thy paths (Pr 3:5-6).

Thou wilt keep him in perfect peace, **whose mind is stayed on thee**: because he trusteth in thee (Isa 26:3).

For, behold, I create new heavens and a new earth: and the former shall not be remembered, **nor come into mind** (Isa 65:17).

Jesus said unto him, Thou shalt love the Lord thy God with all thy heart, and with all thy soul, and **with all thy mind** (Mt 22:37).

And seek not ye what ye shall eat, or what ye shall drink**, neither be ye of doubtful mind** (Lk 12:29).

For to be carnally minded is death; but to be **spiritually minded** is life and peace (Ro 8:6).

For who hath known the mind of the Lord, that he may instruct him? But we have the **mind of Christ** (1Co 2:16).

Let this **mind** be in you, which was also in Christ Jesus (Php 2:5).

Looking unto **Jesus** the author and finisher of our faith; who for the joy that was set before him endured the cross, despising the shame, and is set down at the right hand of the throne of God. For

consider him that endured such contradiction of sinners against himself, **lest ye be wearied and faint in your minds** (Heb 12:2-3).

For God hath not given us the spirit of fear; but of power, and of love, and of a **sound mind** (2Ti 1:7).

Beloved, I wish above all things that thou mayest prosper and be in health, even **as thy soul prospereth** (3Jn 1:2).

Wherefore **gird up the loins of your mind, be sober**, and hope to the end for the grace that is to be brought unto you at the revelation of Jesus Christ (1Pe 1:13).

Promises for Stability

HE WHO dwells in the secret place of the Most High shall remain **stable and fixed** under the shadow of the Almighty [Whose power no foe can withstand] (Ps 91:1 *AMP*).

The [uncompromisingly] righteous shall flourish like the palm tree [be long-lived, stately, upright, useful, and fruitful]; they shall grow like a cedar in Lebanon [majestic, **stable, durable**, and incorruptible] (Ps 92:12 *AMP*).

He shall not be afraid of evil tidings: his heart is **fixed**, trusting in the Lord (Ps 112:7).

God is supremely esteemed. His center holds. Zion brims over with all that is just and right. God keeps your days **stable and secure**— salvation, wisdom,

and knowledge in surplus, and best of
all, Zion's treasure, Fear-of-God (Isa 33:5
THE MESSAGE).

For David says in regard to Him, I saw
the Lord constantly before me, for He is
at my right hand that I may **not be
shaken** or overthrown or cast down
[from my secure and happy state] (Ac
2:25 *AMP*).

Now we beseech you, brethren, by the
coming of our Lord Jesus Christ, and by
our gathering together unto him,
That ye be **not soon shaken in mind**, or
be troubled, neither by spirit, nor by
word, nor by letter as from us, as that
the day of Christ is at hand (2Th 2:1-2).

Suzanne Williams is a native Floridian, wife, mother, daughter, sister, granddaughter, dachshund owner, spelling whiz, wildlife enthusiast, photographer, writer, and child of God whom Christ freed from fear.

To connect with her on the web, visit: http://suzanne-williams-photography.blogspot.com

Made in the USA
Charleston, SC
19 November 2011